# MAKE it WORK!
# RIVERS

Andrew Haslam

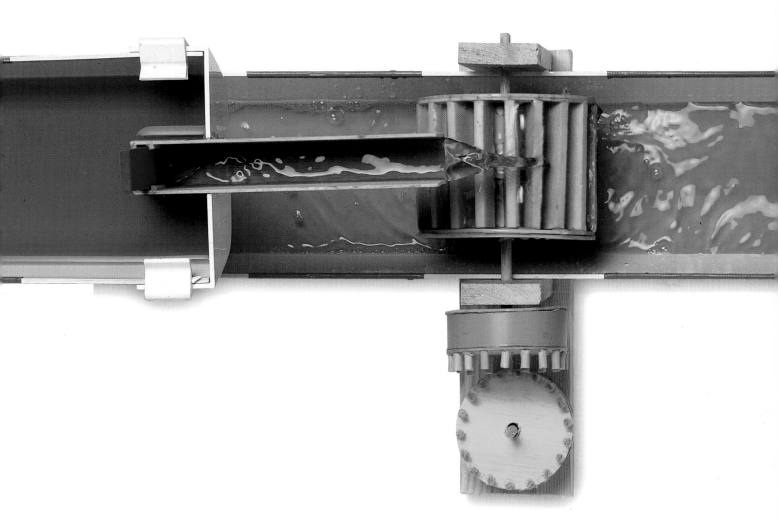

*Consultant*: Dr Geraldene Wharton BSc, PhD

PRINCETON ■ LONDON

Published in the United States and Canada by
Two-Can Publishing LLC
234 Nassau Street
Princeton, NJ 08542

www.two-canpublishing.com

© 2001, 1997 Two-Can Publishing
Design © 1997 Andrew Haslam

For information on Two-Can books and multimedia,
call 1-609-921-6700, fax 1-609-921-3349, or visit our Web site at
http://www.two-canpublishing.com

Created by
act-two
346 Old Street
London EC1V 9RB

Text: Barbara Taylor
Editor: Jacqueline McCann
Art Director: Carole Orbell
Senior Designer: Helen McDonagh
Managing Editor: Christine Morley
Deputy Art Director: Jill Plank
Production: Joya Bart-Plange
Commissioned photography: Jon Barnes and Matthew Ward
Picture Research: Debbie Dorman and Dipika Palmer-Jenkins
Model-makers: Melanie Williams, Peter Griffiths, Paul Holzherr
Thanks to the models: Matthew, Vanisha and Zakkiyah

hc: ISBN 1-58728-256-9
sc: ISBN 1-58728-252-6

hc: 1 2 3 4 5 6 7 8 9 10 02 01
sc: 1 2 3 4 5 6 7 8 9 10 02 01

Photographic credits:
Britstock-Ifa/Jean-Pierre Vollrath p21; Britstock-Ifa/Jim Nelson p27; Bruce Coleman/Atlantide p35;
Bruce Colemen/Charlie Ott p9, p14; Bruce Coleman/Jeff Foott Productions p44;
David Parker/Science Photo Library p24; G.S.F. Picture Library p11; Harvey Maps Ltd p4, p13;
Nic Dunlop/Panos Pictures p30; Oxford Scientific Films/Paul McCullagh p16;
Planet Earth Pictures/Andre Bartschi p32; Robert Harding/Michael Jenner p22;
Survival Anglia/Tony Bomford p10; Zefa p42

Every effort has been made to acknowledge correctly and contact the source
and/or copyright holder of each picture, and Two-Can Publishing apologises for any
unintentional errors or omissions which will be corrected in future editions of this book.

'Two-Can' is a trademark of Two-Can Publishing.
Two-Can Publishing is a division of Zenith Entertainment Ltd,
43-45 Dorset Street, London W1H 4AB

Printed in Hong Kong by Wing King Tong

# Contents

Being a geographer 4

Rivers of the world 6

The water cycle 8

Sources of rivers 10

Drainage patterns 12

Underground rivers 14

The upper river 16

Waterfalls and rapids 20

Energy from the river 22

Dams and reservoirs 24

Lakes and basins 26

River canyons 28

The middle river 30

The human water cycle 36

Farming on the lower river 38

River deltas 40

Flood control 42

Managing rivers 44

Glossary 46

Definitions of words printed in **boldface** in text.

Index 48

# Being a geographer

Geography helps us to understand what happened to the Earth in the past, how it is changing now, and what might happen to it in the future. To try to make sense of our world, geographers study features of the Earth, such as rivers, rocks, oceans and the weather. This is called physical geography.

### What is geography?

Geography is a science of the Earth. It is not only about the physical features that shape our world, but also about the human ones. Geographers look at how people use land for things like settlement, farming, shopping and transport. This is called human geography. They also gather information by studying maps, aerial and satellite photographs and computer databases. In this way, geographers can suggest how best to use the land now and in the future.

▷ *A map and a compass are just some of the tools that geographers use.*

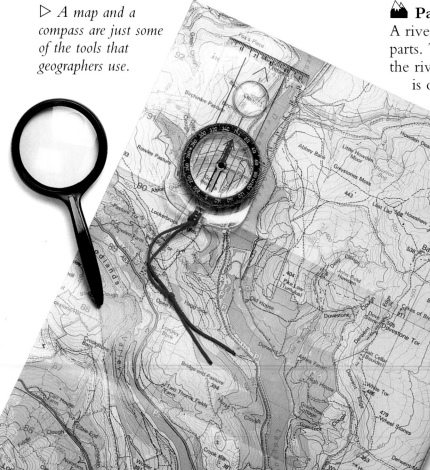

### Geography of rivers

Rivers are an important and powerful force in shaping the land. They carve out **river valleys**, slopes and cliffs by a process called **erosion**. They also carry away rocks, sand and mud, and leave them in other places where they fill in lakes, or build up rich farming land. In this book we will look at rivers and some of the features that you might find along them, such as waterfalls, caves and **meanders**.

### Key to geography symbols

Geographers have to cover a range of topics in their studies. We have introduced symbols where the text refers mainly to important themes. They will help as you read through the book.

| | | | |
|---|---|---|---|
| 📊 **statistics** | | 🌀 energy | |
| ⛰ physical | | 🗻 rock types, or **geology** | |
| ☁ weather | | 👥 human | |

### ⛰ Parts of the river

A river can be roughly divided into three main parts. The first part starts from the source of the river and is called the **upper river**. This is often in the mountains where there are steep valleys, rushing water and narrow streams.

The second part is the **middle river**. Here, the valley is wider and deeper, and so is the river. The river carries more sand, gravel and mud, or **sediment**, than it did in the upper river.

The last stage is the **lower river**. The river winds slowly over a broad, flat plain, dropping some of the sediment it is carrying. Eventually, the river flows into the sea or a lake.

granite
(hard rock)

sandstone
(soft rock)

slate
(hard rock)

### 🏔 Reading rocks

The shape of the land also depends on the rocks under the ground. Some are soft and easily worn away by the wind, rivers or rain. Other rocks are hard and stand out as mountains or hills. Geologists are people who study rocks. Geographers must also study rocks and soil to understand the forces that shape the land.

△ *Geographers often study rock samples from an area.*

### Make it Work!

The Make it Work! way of looking at geography is to carry out experiments and make things that help you understand how geographical processes work. By studying the models and following the step-by-step instructions for the experiments, you will be able to see how rivers work.

You may need to use sharp tools for some of the experiments in the book. Always be careful and ask an adult to help you.

▷ *By studying rivers, geographers can help prevent damage to people and property from flooding.*

### Geographers' tools

Geographers use maps to study changes in the landscape, to look at human settlement, or simply to find their way from place to place. A compass shows which direction to take. A small hammer and brush are useful for breaking off and dusting small pieces of rock to identify. They are also useful if you are looking for **fossils** hidden in rocks. Take photographs or make sketches of the features and things you see, so that you can record them accurately.

△ *Photographs are a useful way of recording how places change over time.*

# Rivers of the world

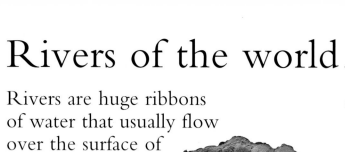

Rivers are huge ribbons of water that usually flow over the surface of the land. All rivers flow in a shallow trench or channel they have cut in the ground. On average, about 5,600 cubic miles of water flow down the world's rivers each year—enough water to cover all dry land in a layer 12 inches deep. Each year, rivers carry away about 22 billion tons of rocks, soil and sand from the land and dump it into the sea or into lakes.

## Rivers past and present

Some of the world's largest cities have grown along the banks, or at the mouths of important rivers. Shanghai sprang up on the Yangtze River in China; New York, in the U.S., is at the mouth of the Hudson River and is an important port; and Cairo, the largest city in Africa, has stood on the banks of the Nile for over a thousand years.

People all over the world live near rivers because they need them for water, farming, industry and transport. Although rivers are useful to people, they can be dangerous. When rivers flood, they can cause damage to crops and property and great loss of life—especially to people who live on **deltas**.

North America

Lake Superior is the largest freshwater lake in the world.

St. Louis

New Orleans

The Mississippi flows for 2,340 mi. into the Gulf of Mexico.

Manaus

Angel Falls is the world's highest waterfall at 3,212 ft.

South America

The source of the Amazon River is in the Andes Mountains in Peru.

The banks of the Amazon Delta are farther apart than London and Paris.

One-fifth of the fresh water in all the Earth's rivers flows in the Amazon.

▷ These symbols are used to locate some of the world's largest cities, deltas and waterfalls.

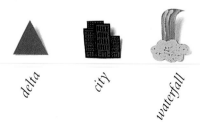

delta    city    waterfall

△ This map shows the world's largest rivers and some of the cities that are found along them.

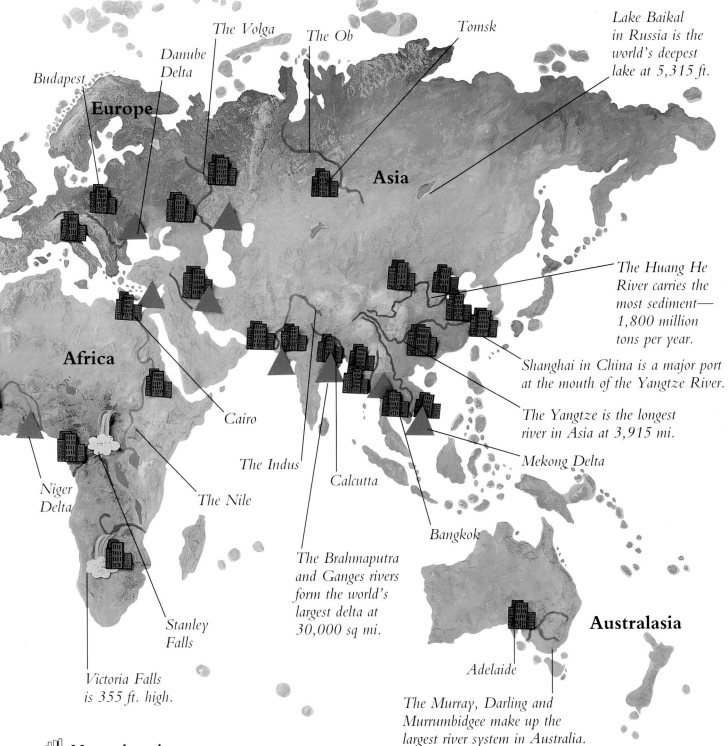

Budapest

Europe

The Volga

Danube Delta

The Ob

Tomsk

Lake Baikal in Russia is the world's deepest lake at 5,315 ft.

Asia

The Huang He River carries the most sediment—1,800 million tons per year.

Shanghai in China is a major port at the mouth of the Yangtze River.

The Yangtze is the longest river in Asia at 3,915 mi.

Mekong Delta

Africa

Cairo

The Indus

Calcutta

Niger Delta

The Nile

Bangkok

Stanley Falls

The Brahmaputra and Ganges rivers form the world's largest delta at 30,000 sq mi.

Australasia

Victoria Falls is 355 ft. high.

Adelaide

The Murray, Darling and Murrumbidgee make up the largest river system in Australia.

## 𝚤𝚤𝚤 Measuring rivers

Rivers are not only bodies of water—they also carry huge quantities of sediment that help to shape the landscape. To measure a river's power to eat into the land and carry it away, geographers calculate the amount of water in the river, and the speed at which it flows.

Geographers work out how much rain falls into rivers, and how much soaks into the soil. A lot of the rain that falls on the land eventually finds its way into rivers, so it is important to know how much rain falls, and how much water the soil can hold.

# The water cycle

The water cycle is the never-ending movement of water between the land, the sea and the **atmosphere**. Rivers contain less than 1 per cent of all the fresh water on Earth, yet they form a vital part of this cycle.

**How water is recycled**
The sun heats the water in rivers, lakes, oceans and plants. The water evaporates, which means that it changes into **water vapor**. Water vapor rises because it weighs less than cold air. High in the sky, the vapor cools and changes back into drops of liquid water. This is called condensation. The drops gather together to make clouds and eventually fall as rain, hail or snow. The cycle then starts all over again.

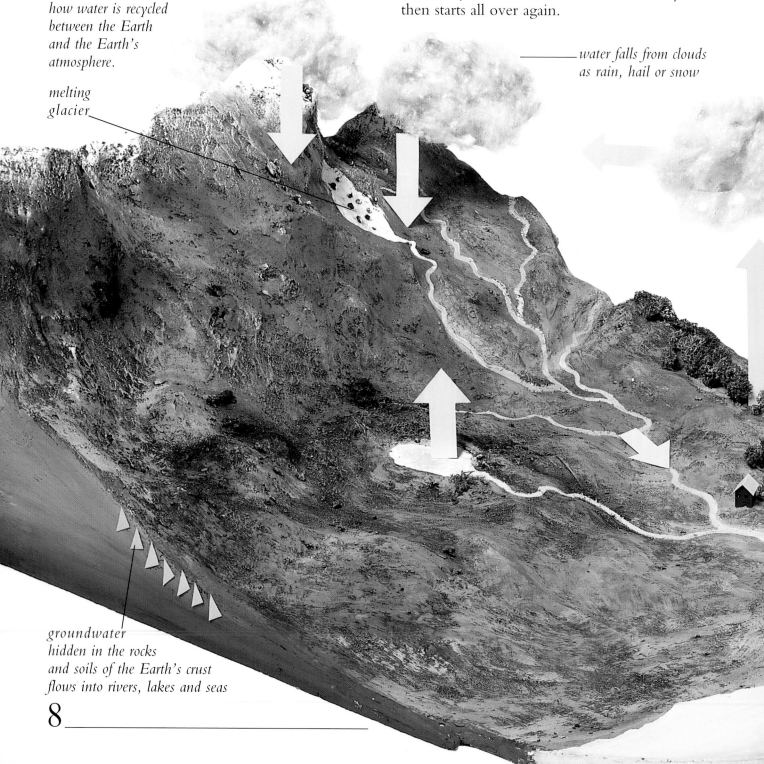

▽ *This model shows how water is recycled between the Earth and the Earth's atmosphere.*

*melting glacier*

—————*water falls from clouds as rain, hail or snow*

*groundwater hidden in the rocks and soils of the Earth's crust flows into rivers, lakes and seas*

△ *Rainfall is often heaviest in the mountains where the air temperature is cooler. This causes the water vapor to condense and fall as rain, hail or snow.*

### ⛰ Forms of water

Water exists in three forms: liquid water in rivers, lakes or the sea; water vapor, which is invisible gas in the air; and solid water, or ice, which is in glaciers and frozen rivers, lakes, ponds or seas.

### ⛅ A freshwater supply

The Earth's water is constantly recycled, so the amount of water on Earth always stays the same. However, 97 per cent of all the Earth's water is salty and makes up the oceans and seas. Most of the fresh water is frozen in ice sheets and glaciers at the North and South Poles and in mountains, so we cannot use it. But when water evaporates from the sea, the salt is left behind. This means that the water vapor in the atmosphere, which condenses and falls as rain, is fresh water.

### CREATE A WATER CYCLE

**You will need** sheet of glass, 12 bricks, hardboard, plastic tray, boiling water (kettle)

**1** Position the bricks, glass, tray and hardboard as shown. The bricks represent mountains, the tray is the sea, the glass is the atmosphere and the hardboard is land.

**2** Ask an adult to boil some water in a kettle and pour it into the tray. (We added food coloring to show what happens more clearly.)

**Result:** steam rises from the hot water. This shows how the heat of the sun makes water evaporate and form rain clouds over land or sea. When the steam hits the cold glass, the water condenses and droplets form (rain). The water falls onto the hardboard and runs down the slope (river) toward the tray (sea).

clouds made of millions of droplets of water or ice suspended in the sky

water condenses and forms clouds

water evaporates from land and sea

# Sources of rivers

The beginning of a river is called its source. Many of the world's biggest rivers begin in natural hollows in the land. Water trickles in from the surrounding soil to form a tiny flow of water called a seep. Even huge rivers, such as the Nile in Egypt or the Amazon in South America, start from small sources like this. Other rivers flow from a marsh or a lake, or from the end of a slowly melting glacier in the mountains.

△ In marshes such as this one in Ireland, the soil is water-logged and covered with plants that hold a lot of water in their roots, leaves and stems.

**DRAINAGE TEST**

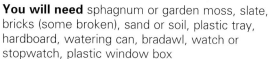

**You will need** sphagnum or garden moss, slate, bricks (some broken), sand or soil, plastic tray, hardboard, watering can, bradawl, watch or stopwatch, plastic window box

**1** Make a hole at the bottom of one side of the tray with the bradawl. Fill the tray with moss. Position the tray, bricks, window box and hardboard as shown above. The hole in the tray should sit just over the hardboard, at the end close to the window box.

**2** Fill the watering can, then pour the water evenly over the moss. Time how long it takes for the water to filter through the moss and trickle down the board. You should find that the moss, which is found in marshy areas or peat bogs, holds water very well.

**3** Repeat the experiment with soil or sand in the tray. You will notice that the water carries some of the sand with it. This shows how the river wears away **sedimentary rock**, which does not hold water as well as sphagnum moss, and carries it farther downstream.

#### 🏔 Water drainage

Some rocks such as chalk and limestone, have pores, cracks and joints in them that let water drain easily. These are **permeable** rocks. Rocks that do not let water pass through them are impermeable. The size of the particles in rocks and the way they are arranged affect how permeable they are.

## ⛰ Springs, glaciers and marshes

Sometimes water collects underground. It runs over impermeable rocks until it finds a way out and surfaces as a spring. Many rivers begin as mountain springs.

Glaciers are "rivers of ice." They form when snow is squashed into ice that is so thick and heavy that it slides slowly downhill. The tip of a glacier is called a snout or a lip. When the snout melts, it may become the source of a river.

In marshes and other wetland areas, the soil is often made of peat. Peaty soil is made of plants that have partly rotted down. They hold a lot of water that may eventually be released to supply a river.

△ *The Indus, Ganges and Mekong are three of Asia's largest rivers. Their sources are high in the Himalayan mountains, in glaciers like this one.*

**4** See what happens in a limestone region by arranging some broken bricks in the tray, as above. The gaps between the bricks represent the natural joints found in rock. Now pour on the water. The water does not pass through the bricks, but it drains well through the cracks.

**5** Finally, place a piece of slate on top of the bricks. Pour water onto the slate and measure the time it takes for it to run off. The slate does not absorb any water as it is impermeable, so the water runs off very quickly. This is what happens in an area of hard, impermeable rock.

*mica schist (impermeable)*

*limestone (permeable)*

*slate (impermeable)*

*granite (impermeable)*

*red sandstone (permeable)*

*pumice (permeable)*

# Drainage patterns

From its source, a river flows downhill. This is because of the Earth's gravity which pulls everything down towards the ground. Small trickles of water join up and form a stream. The amount of water in the stream increases steadily as more streams, called **tributaries**, join it. Eventually, the stream becomes big enough to be called a river.

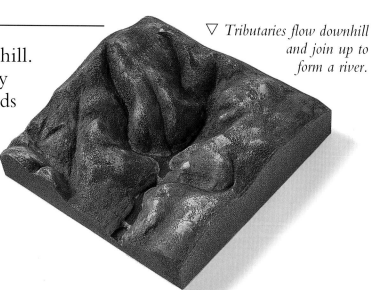

▽ *Tributaries flow downhill and join up to form a river.*

## MAKE A DRAINAGE PATTERN

**You will need** contour map with rivers, scissors, ruler, strips of paper, pen, graph paper, plasticine, stickers

**1** Select a river and six tributaries.

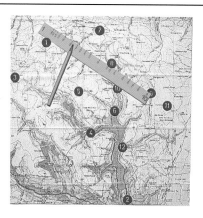

**2** Number the stickers. Place the first one at the source of a tributary and the second where the tributary joins the main river. Cut a strip of paper the same length as the tributary. Copy the sticker numbers onto each end of the strip. Do this for all the tributaries and the river.

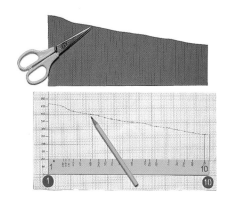

**3** Match each strip to its tributary. Copy the **contour lines** and the height every 50 yds. on the strip.

**4** Plot a scale on graph paper from the lowest to the highest point (0=sea level). Place each strip on the graph. Plot the height to create a profile.

### ⛰ Supplying the river

A **drainage basin** is all the land that supplies a river and its tributaries with water (see page 17). If you could look down on a river from above, you would see that it branches. This is called a **drainage pattern**. The shape of the pattern depends on rocks, soil, climate and the changes made to the river. Radial drainage occurs when streams flow down from a central high point, such as a mountain top. Other rivers, such as the Amazon, form a pattern like the branches of a tree. This is called dendritic drainage.

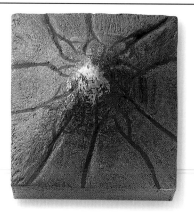

*radial drainage*

*dendritic drainage*

Rivers and their tributaries can form many other types of drainage patterns.

Parallel drainage occurs when streams flow in valleys that are parallel to one another. This might be because movements in the Earth, millions of years ago, made the rocks "fold" into parallel lines.

Trellis drainage is common where massive layers of sedimentary rock have "slipped." Streams flow in channels that are parallel to each other, and tributaries join the streams at right angles.

*parallel drainage*  *trellis drainage*

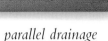

**5** Copy the river profile onto colored paper and cut it out. Do this for each tributary and the main river.

**6** Fix each profile to the river and its tributaries with plasticine. Does the pattern on your map match any of the drainage patterns shown here?

▷ *This is the drainage pattern of the landscape model at the top of the opposite page.*

**Comparing rivers**
By measuring river profiles, drainage patterns and rainfall, geographers can study how much water flows down a river. This helps them to predict when most water will flow in the river and also to compare rivers from different areas (see page 18).

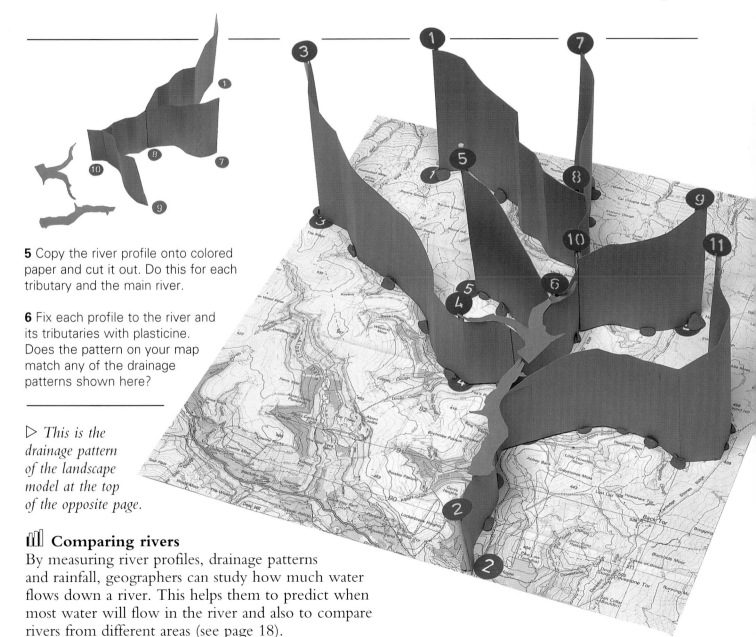

# Underground rivers

As water seeps underground, it can eat into soft, permeable rock such as limestone, forming caves and river channels. Rainwater is slightly acidic and, over time, dissolves away the rock. The water seeps into the natural cracks and joints in limestone and enlarges the gaps by slowly dissolving the rock.

*1 talc*
*(fingernail)*

*2 gypsum*
*(fingernail)*

*3 calcite*
*(copper coin)*

### Underground water

Rivers can also form under the ground in places where rocks are so full of water they cannot hold any more. The top of a layer of water-logged rock is called the **water table**. If the water table reaches above ground level, a spring appears. Underground pockets of water held in rocks are called **aquifers**.

### Mohs scale

About 180 years ago, a German geologist called Friedrich Mohs worked out a way of arranging minerals in order of hardness. He invented a scale from 1–10, called Mohs scale. The softest mineral, talc, is 1 on the scale and the hardest, diamond, is 10. Each mineral will scratch those below it on the scale, and will be scratched by those above it.

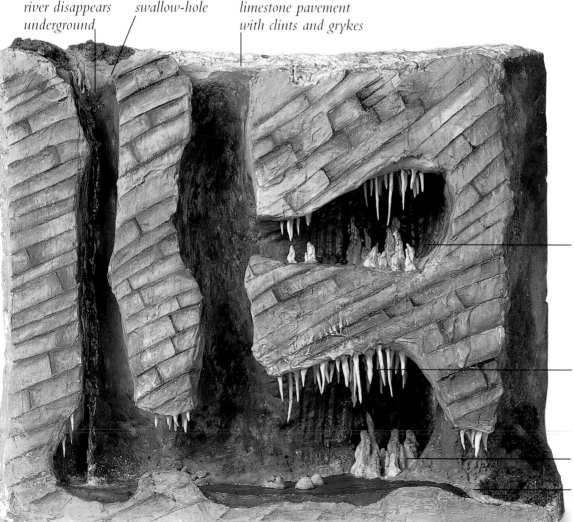

*river disappears underground*

*swallow-hole*

*limestone pavement with clints and grykes*

◁ *Underground caves are mostly caused by water eroding rock—either in coastal areas, or in limestone regions.*

*cave hollowed out by water*

***stalactites** grow about 10 in. in 500 years*

***stalagmites***

*river reappears where water table reaches ground level*

*4 fluorite*       *5 apatite*      *6 orthoclase*
               *(penknife)*    *(window glass)*

◁ *Mohs scale is based on these 10 minerals. Here, some of them are compared to everyday objects of equal hardness.*

*7 quartz*    *8 topaz*     *9*    *10*
*(steel knife)* *(sandpaper)* *corundum* *diamond*

### 🏔 Rocks and minerals

Rocks are usually made from mixtures of building blocks called minerals. Gold, copper and diamond are all minerals, and so is talc, which is used to make talcum powder. Other minerals have more unusual names such as corundum or apatite. Chalk and limestone are made of calcite, and granite is made of the minerals quartz, feldspar and mica.

Chalk is a **porous** rock. This means that it has many small air spaces, or pores, which hold water like a sponge. Chalk is also permeable: it lets water drain through the gaps in it.

△ *If the roof of a cave collapses, a larger cave called a cavern is formed. This is Carlsbad Caverns in N.M.*

### 🏔 Limestone regions

As water flows over an area of limestone rock, it enlarges the natural cracks and joints, forming a limestone pavement. The grooves are called grykes and the blocks between them are called clints. When the water disappears underground, a hole called a swallow-hole forms. These holes can eventually grow into large potholes.

Many underground caves are found in places where the rock is mostly limestone. As water drips down from the roofs in limestone caves, it dissolves the minerals in the rocks. At the same time, the dripping water evaporates, leaving the minerals behind. These build up, over hundreds of years, into stalactites, which hang down from the roof, and stalagmites, which grow up from the ground. Sometimes they meet in the middle and form a pillar.

### MAKE A STALACTITE _____

**You will need** paper clips, two glasses, washing soda crystals, string, saucer, distilled water

**1** Half-fill both glasses with distilled water and gradually pour in as many soda crystals as the water will dissolve.

**2** Dip a length of string in the solution. Run it between both glasses, securing with paper clips. Place a saucer between the glasses and leave for three or four days.

**Result:** the solution travels along the string as if it were the roof of a cave. When the solution reaches the lowest point, it drips onto the saucer. The water evaporates, leaving soda deposits that form a hanging soda stalactite. In a few more days, a soda stalagmite will also grow in the saucer.

# The upper river

The way rivers shape the land depends on how fast they flow and the kinds of rocks they flow over. In its upper course in the mountains, the river carves out a narrow, steep-sided valley that is usually in the shape of the letter V. The riverbed has a steep slope, or gradient, and the water cuts down into the land because the force of the water breaks up the rocks beneath it. Loose pebbles, stones and bits of grit bounce along the river bottom, rubbing against the rocks and wearing them away even more.

◁ *interlocking spurs*

▽ *truncated spurs*

### 🏔 Spurs
Typical features of the upper river valley are "tongues" of land that stick out into the valley. These are called **interlocking spurs**. The river winds around these spurs because they are made of hard rock.

Eventually the river may wear away the tips of the spurs, so that they become blunted instead of pointed. These are called truncated spurs.

△ *Braided rivers, like this one in Bhutan, occur in many places, although they are more common where the sediment is coarse and slopes are steep.*

### 🏔 Braided rivers
Braided rivers look rather like a braid in a person's hair. They appear in places where valley slopes are steep, or in dry areas where there is a lot of sand and gravel. The river threads its way around bars of gravel, sand and other coarse sediment. In the upper river, braiding usually occurs where a river works loose a lot of material that it cannot carry away.

▽ *In its upper course, the river takes up most of the narrow valley floor, winding around obstacles and eroding the steep valley sides.*

*boulders carried down by the river in times of flood when the river has great power*

*very little flat land for people to build homes, farms or roads*

*braided channels wind around bars of coarse material*

## Land shapes

The upper river often runs through deep, narrow valleys with interlocking or truncated spurs. Wide, flat-topped mountains or hills lie between the valleys. The river is too shallow for transporting goods or people easily. It is also difficult to build roads or railroads across the river, although this has been done in the European Alps and the Andes of South America.

*V-shaped valley with steep sides*

*tributaries*

## Uses of the upper river

The steep valley sides make it difficult to grow crops, although animals can graze on them. **Dams** and **reservoirs** are often built on the upper river because it is easy to block the water here and distribute it to people downstream (see pages 24-25).

*rivers often begin in the mountains where there is a lot of rain*

*waterfall*

*drainage basin*

*broad hilltop forms a dividing line between two drainage basins*

*drainage basin*

*the river cuts downwards through hard rock to make a steep-sided gorge*

# The upper river

### 📊 Looking at rivers in profile
Geographers look at profiles of rivers to compare the way they flow at different points along their length. Rivers always move from higher areas down to lower ones. They usually begin with a fairly steep fall, then slope more gently as they continue their journey down, before flattening out as they finally reach the sea.

▷ *This is a profile of the Amazon River which is 4,000 miles long. Each marker on the base represents 100 miles. Geographers compare rivers from different areas by making profiles like this.*

### 📊 The mighty Amazon
The Amazon has an unusual profile. From its source in the Andes, it plunges down the mountainsides, dropping 5,470 yards in its first 620 miles. Then it runs almost level, dropping only 4 inches every 1.8 miles, as it winds across South America. It is so powerful that it carries sediment 60 miles out to sea and pours five times more water into the sea than any other river.

## RIVER LOAD EXPERIMENT

**You will need** bowl, wooden spoon, jug of water, coarse sand

**1** Place all the sand in the bowl and then pour in the water.

**2** Stir the water quickly with the wooden spoon, without touching the sand. You will see that the moving water picks up the sand particles, or sediment, and moves them around.

**3** Remove the spoon and let the water settle. The large particles of sand should sink first (they are heavier). As the water slows, the smaller particles settle. Only moving water will carry any particles.

## MAKE A SEDIMENT MEASURE

**You will need** two long strips and six small strips of wood, plasticine, three jars with screw-top lids, acrylic paint, glue, plastic tubing, three funnels, three rubber bands, piece of muslin

**1** Make two holes in the jar lid. Push the neck of the funnel into one hole and a short length of plastic tubing into the other. Secure them both with plasticine.

**2** Use a rubber band to fix a small piece of muslin over the plastic tube, on the inside of the lid. Then screw the lid on the jar. The funnel lets the water and sediment in; the tube lets the water out. Make two more sediment measures in the same way.

**3** Measure the width of your jars. Then make a ladder from the pieces of wood, as shown and paint. The rungs and rails must be wide enough apart for you to wedge in the jars at different levels along the ladder.

**4** Rest your sediment measure upright in a shallow stream in the opposite direction to the flow of the river (one jar should rest on the riverbed). After an hour, remove the measure and unscrew the lids. Compare the type of sediment and the amount collected in each of the jars.

**Result:** the jar at the bottom should contain coarse sediment that moves by jumping along the riverbed. A river's **load** is heaviest near the riverbed. The top jar should contain finer particles of sediment. This is because the water nearer the top of the river travels faster than the water at the bottom and carries lighter particles.

## ⛰ The power of a river

The power of a river is so great that it can erode the land and change its shape. But this depends on the type of channel it flows along and the type of material, or load, it picks up and carries to the sea. It also depends on how much water the river contains, how fast it is moving and how steeply the land slopes down to sea level.

▽ *The measure can tell us how much, and what type of sediment is in the river.*

## ⛰ Eroding the land

The water in rivers has some important effects on the shape of the land. First, as it flows through the river channel, water can dissolve minerals in the rocks so that they disappear and are carried away. Second, water can push into cracks and crevices, breaking off bits of rock and mud along the riverbank.

Third, rivers wear away the land by a process called abrasion. This is when the river's load scratches and scrapes against rocks and soil in the channel. Fourthly, the load itself is broken down into smaller particles. This process is called attrition. The effect of abrasion and attrition is to wear away the riverbed and riverbanks, making them wider and deeper.

## ⛰ Moving the load

Most of a river's load is moved during short periods of heavy flooding. The river carries its load in three ways. Particles of stones, gravel and coarse sand, called the bedload, move along the riverbed by rolling, tumbling or bouncing downstream in small jerks and jumps. As one particle lands, it bumps into another, making it hop along the riverbed. This jumping movement is called saltation.

Other tiny particles of fine sand and **silt** hang or float in the water. These are called the suspended load. Some materials dissolve in the water. This is the dissolved, or solution load.

# Waterfalls and rapids

Waterfalls and rapids are often found along the upper river. A waterfall occurs where a river falls steeply over a band of hard rock, often making a deep pool as it hits softer rock below. **Rapids** are stretches of fast-flowing water tumbling over a rocky, shallow riverbed.

### 🏔 A thousand-year process

If a river flows over hard and then soft rock, it wears away the softer rock first, leaving a small step of hard rock sticking up into the river. Over thousands of years, the soft rock is worn away until eventually the river falls from a great height.

▽ Eventually the hard rock is eroded and a new waterfall forms farther upstream.

△ The soft rock below the hard rock is worn away over time to form a waterfall.

water falls over a vertical layer of hard rock

plunge pool

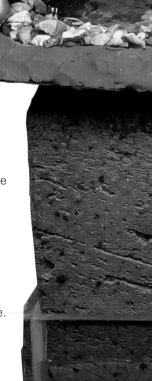

## MAKE A WATERFALL

**You will need** glass tank or water container, six bricks, three small tiles, small stones (shingle), large stones, plasticine, slate or large tile, jug, water

**1** Set up the bricks and tank as shown. Balance the slate on the bricks in the tank. Use the remaining bricks to support the slate at the other end.

**2** Put a layer of shingle in the glass tank. For rapids, lay the small tiles at an angle to the shingle, facing the waterfall. Secure with large stones and plasticine.

**3** Make raised banks on the sides of the slate using plasticine, shingle and stones. Pour water onto the slate.

**Result:** the water runs over the waterfall, making a plunge pool as it swirls around and shifts the shingle. The water should froth as it hits the tiles, or rapids.

## ⛰ Waterfalls of the world

Not all waterfalls and rapids are created by rivers alone. Some are made when movements in the Earth's crust push up a cliff or rock; others are formed by glaciers. Some waterfalls form on cliffs near the coast, or even under the sea, where the seabed is pushed up to make underwater steps. In fact, the world's biggest waterfall is under the sea between Greenland and Iceland—the water falls an amazing 2 miles. The highest waterfall on the Earth's surface is Angel Falls in Venezuela which is 3,212 feet high.

## ⛰ Plunge pools

Plunge pools are found in soft rock at the bottom of some waterfalls. They are deep pools, carved out by boulders and stones that are whirled around by the huge force of the falling water.

## ⛰ Rapids and cataracts

Cataracts are series of rapids that form where bands of hard rock are tilted at an angle to the river. The rocks break up the flow, but are not big enough to form a waterfall. White, frothy water appears on top of cataracts in shallow areas.

△ *The water over rapids and cataracts foams and splashes to make patches of "white water." This canoeist faces the challenge of the rapids in a deep gorge in Austria.*

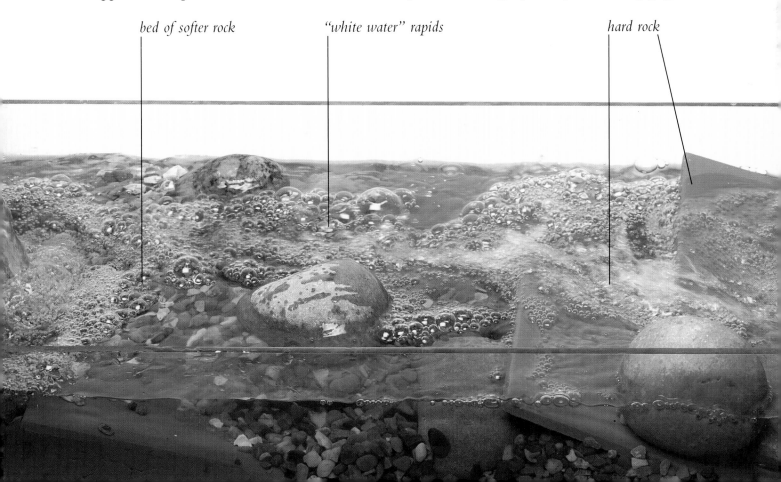

*bed of softer rock*          *"white water" rapids*          *hard rock*

# Energy from the river

Flowing water is an endless source of energy. People have used water energy for thousands of years by placing water wheels in rivers. The water provides the wheels with the energy to turn the millstones that grind grain. In many countries, water wheels are used to lift water from the river to **irrigate** crops.

▷ *These ancient water wheels on the Orontes River in Syria are still used to irrigate nearby fields.*

## MAKE A WATER WHEEL

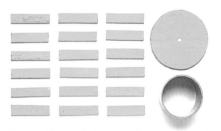

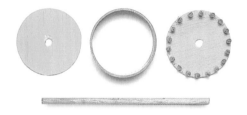

**You will need:** length of rain gutter, four gutter stops, piece of drainpipe, bricks, balsa wood, soft wood (pine), bradawl, washer, matchsticks, jug, water, hand drill, glue, $1/6$ in. dowel, craft knife (ask an adult to help you when cutting)

**1** The wheel: cut two balsa circles, 4 in. across. Make a $1/5$ in. hole in the center of each. For paddles, cut 18 balsa rectangles, 2 x $1/3$ in.

**2** Glue the paddles to one circle as shown. Glue a piece of drainpipe, 2 in. long x 3 in. in diameter, in the middle of the paddles. Glue on the final circle.

**3** The cogs: cut a 1 in. length of drainpipe. Cut two balsa circles, 2 in. across. Make a $1/5$ in. hole in each. Glue to each side of the drainpipe. Cut 18 pieces of dowel $1/3$ in. long.

**4** Glue the dowel pieces around one of the circles, as shown above. Make a second cog following steps 3 and 4.

**5** The water-wheel support: cut one piece of pine 10 x 3 in. Cut two more, 6 x 3 in. and make two $1/5$ in. holes at the top center of each. The support must be wide and tall enough to surround the gutter.

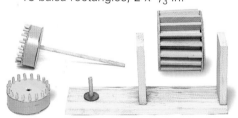
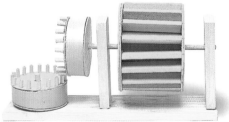
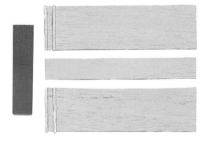

**6** Glue the pieces together as shown above. Then, cut an 8 in. length of dowel. Glue a cog to the end of it. Slide the dowel through the hole in the upright, the water-wheel and the second upright.

**7** Place the second cog on the base so that its teeth mesh with the water-wheel cog. Mark position on base.

**8** Remove the cog and drill a small hole over the mark. Cut a 1 in. length of dowel and push it into the hole in the base. Put a washer over the dowel, as shown above left.

**9** Replace the second cog so that it rests on the washer. The teeth of both cogs should mesh together comfortably.

**10** Cut four lengths of balsa wood: one 5 x $3/4$ in.; one $5/8$ x 3 in.; two 5 x $1 1/2$ in. Glue four matchsticks across the two large pieces ($1/10$ in. apart) as shown above.

**11** Glue the pieces together to make a long, narrow, open-ended box. Slide the shortest piece of wood (sluice gate) between the matchsticks.

**12** Cut a long piece of rain gutter and slide it through the support for the water wheel. Seal off the ends of the rain gutter with gutter stops.

**13** Cut a second length of rain gutter and seal with gutter stops. Rest it on top of the first rain gutter using the bricks as supports. Cut a gap in one gutter stop, small enough for the trough to slide in. Finally, pour water into the top rain gutter and let it flow onto the water wheel. By raising and lowering the sluice gate you can control the flow of water.

### ✻ Under or over—which is best?

In an undershot water wheel, water pushes the paddles around from below. In an overshot wheel, the water falls onto the wheel from above. The overshot wheel is more efficient, because the weight of water held in the paddles gives the wheel more pushing power.

Most water wheels are located on the upper river. This is because the gradient of the river bed is steeper, so the fast-flowing water provides more power, and because the narrow channel makes the wheel more stable in the river.

### ✻ Modern water power

Nowadays, water is used all over the world to generate electricity by turning gigantic water wheels called turbines (see pages 24-25). Modern turbines weigh thousands of tons and are designed to make as much use of the energy from the moving water as possible. They are much more efficient than the original water wheels.

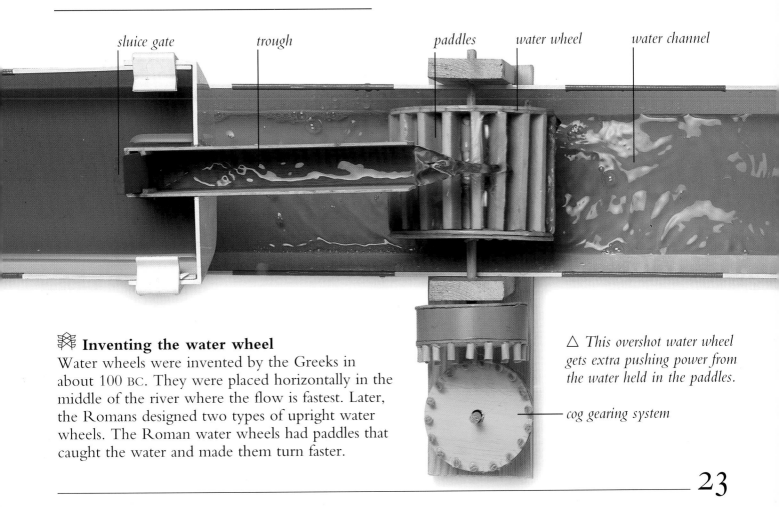

sluice gate    trough    paddles    water wheel    water channel

### ✻ Inventing the water wheel

Water wheels were invented by the Greeks in about 100 BC. They were placed horizontally in the middle of the river where the flow is fastest. Later, the Romans designed two types of upright water wheels. The Roman water wheels had paddles that caught the water and made them turn faster.

△ *This overshot water wheel gets extra pushing power from the water held in the paddles.*

— *cog gearing system*

# Dams and reservoirs

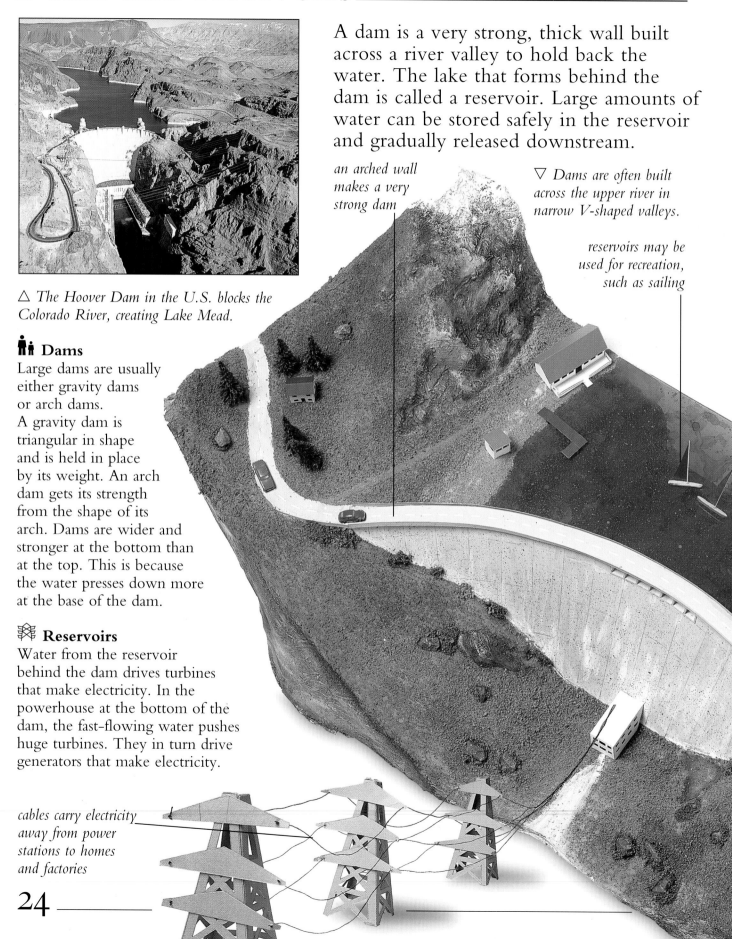

A dam is a very strong, thick wall built across a river valley to hold back the water. The lake that forms behind the dam is called a reservoir. Large amounts of water can be stored safely in the reservoir and gradually released downstream.

*an arched wall makes a very strong dam*

▽ *Dams are often built across the upper river in narrow V-shaped valleys.*

*reservoirs may be used for recreation, such as sailing*

△ *The Hoover Dam in the U.S. blocks the Colorado River, creating Lake Mead.*

## 👥 Dams

Large dams are usually either gravity dams or arch dams. A gravity dam is triangular in shape and is held in place by its weight. An arch dam gets its strength from the shape of its arch. Dams are wider and stronger at the bottom than at the top. This is because the water presses down more at the base of the dam.

## ⚙ Reservoirs

Water from the reservoir behind the dam drives turbines that make electricity. In the powerhouse at the bottom of the dam, the fast-flowing water pushes huge turbines. They in turn drive generators that make electricity.

*cables carry electricity away from power stations to homes and factories*

24

**TEST A DAM**

**You will need** colored tape, large tank, scissors, thick cardboard, plasticine, jug, water

**1** Cut a rectangle of cardboard slightly wider than the tank. Place it in the tank. The cardboard should curve in the middle.

**2** Seal the sides and bottom of the cardboard to the tank with plasticine, so that it is watertight. Next, to measure the water level, cut thin strips of tape and stick them at regular intervals along one side of the tank.

**3** Pour water slowly and steadily into the tank. Take regular readings of the water level. At what point does the cardboard give way under pressure from the water?

### ❋ Hydroelectric power

A power station that uses energy from water to make electricity is called a **hydroelectric power** station. Such stations are often built on the upper river where the valley is narrow and easy to dam, and there is plenty of rainfall. In mountainous countries, such as Switzerland, nearly all the electricity is generated by hydroelectric power.

*roads are sometimes built across the tops of dams*

*water tower*

**4** Make a curved dam with a rectangle of cardboard that is twice the width of the tank. Now, repeat the experiment.

**Result:** the second dam will hold much more water than the first because the dam gets its strength from its greater curved shape.

### ❋ Power stations

Dam walls are high so that the water falls a long way and provides a huge force to drive the turbines that generate electricity. Water is a never-ending source of energy and hydroelectric power stations do not pollute the environment in the way that power stations running on coal or oil do. But changing the natural flow of water in a river can cause a lack of water downstream for people, farms, plants or animals.

# Lakes and basins

Lakes are large hollows, or basins, in the surface of the land. They appear at different places along the length of a river; sometimes they are the source of a river, at other times they are the place where rivers end up. Lakes can be formed by natural forces such as glaciation, movements in the Earth, or even by beavers blocking rivers with twigs and branches. People also create lakes by building dams across rivers.

▷ *Water collects in a natural hollow in the land to form a lake. The water comes from rivers, rainfall, melting snows or rainwater that seeps through soil and rock.*

## Disappearing lakes

Lakes can be almost any size, shape or depth. Some are regular features of the landscape, while others appear only at certain times of the year, perhaps when there are very heavy rains. Lake Eyre in Australia dries up completely in some years and often remains dry for two or three years at a time. The one thing that all lakes have in common is that they do not last forever. The water eventually evaporates, or is drained by rivers, or fills in with plants and soil. Given time, most lakes will turn back into dry land.

*river tributaries*

*main river*

*mud, sand and pebbles carried by the river settle on the edges of the lake*

*beach shows where lake once reached a higher level*

*natural hollow*

*water seeps through soil and rock until it reaches the water table (the top of a layer of water-filled rock)*

△ *This is an erosion lake in Washington state.*

### 🏔 **How are they formed?**

Most lakes are found in hollows that were scooped out by glaciers and ice sheets during the ice ages thousands of years ago. Other lakes formed when rivers were blocked by material left behind by ice sheets or volcanoes. In North America, the huge weight of one ice sheet made the land sink into a basin. After the ice melted, the basin filled with water to form the Great Lakes.

Some of the world's biggest lakes, such as Lake Baikal in Russia, were formed by powerful movements inside the Earth. Earth movements also push volcanoes up from the land. Sometimes the top of a volcano collapses and fills with water to form a crater lake.

### 🏔 **Erosion lakes**

At the start of a mountain glacier, the ice may erode a bowl-shaped hollow in the rock. When the ice melts, the hollow fills up with water to form a round lake, known as an erosion lake. The English Lake District was formed in this way.

### 🏔 **Rift valley lakes**

Forces inside the Earth can cause a block of land to slip downward, making a steep-sided valley called a rift valley. Lake Tanganyika in Africa and Lake Baikal are rift valley lakes. These lakes are long, narrow and very deep—the bottom is often below sea level.

*rift valley lake*

### 🏔 **Barrier lakes**

When glaciers melt, they leave behind rocks, mud and other material. Water collects in hollows, and the rocks and mud stop it from seeping away. Hundreds of small lakes called barrier lakes can form this way. The lake plateau of Finland has many barrier lakes. It is known as "the land of 40,000 lakes."

*barrier lakes*

*erosion lake*

# River canyons

In parts of the world that have long dry seasons, some rivers carve deep valleys called **canyons**. The rivers get their water from mountains far away, or from underground. When rain falls on canyons, it is usually in short, heavy bursts. There is little soil and few plants to soak up the water, so it rushes over the land, carrying loose rocks with it. Two of the world's most spectacular canyons are the Grand Canyon in Arizona and the Nile Canyon in Egypt.

### The world's largest canyon

The Grand Canyon is almost 277 mi. long, up to 18 mi. wide and 1 mi. deep. It takes a whole day to walk to the bottom. The Grand Canyon formed over the past six million years as the land rose and the river cut downwards into it. Layers of hard and soft rock have worn away at different rates. Today, the hard rock stands out as cliffs, while the soft rock has formed slopes.

## How the Grand Canyon was formed

**1** About 2 billion years ago, powerful forces inside the Earth caused layers of sediments and volcanic lava to fold. Slowly, these layers were pushed into a mountain range 5-6 mi. high.

**2** Gradually the mountains were worn away and more sediments built up as seas flooded the land. The land tipped up to form new mountains, but by 600 million years ago, all that remained was a hilly plain.

▷ *The walls of the Grand Canyon have been carved out by wind, rain and the Colorado River.*

*steep-sided valley, or canyon*

*limestone, sandstone and shales*

## EROSION TEST

**3** Pour water slowly into the center of the tank and watch what happens.

**Result:** the water quickly forms a deep pit or canyon in the dry sand. This is roughly how canyons are formed, although the real process takes millions of years!

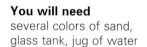

**You will need**
several colors of sand, glass tank, jug of water

**1** Pour the dry sand into the tank, using layers of different colors to represent beds of sedimentary rock.

**2** Add the final layer and make sure it is level.

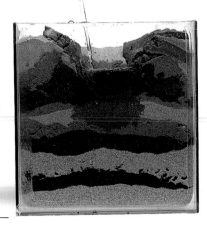

**3** Seas and rivers covered the land again, depositing more sediments up to 1 1/2 mi. thick. This lasted until 65 million years ago.

**4** Over millions of years the layers of rock were worn away. The Colorado River started to drain westward over the area.

**5** In the past few million years, the land has risen and the river has cut down into the layers of ancient rocks to form a canyon.

### Earth history

Walking down the Grand Canyon is like stepping back in time. The limestone rocks found at the top are the most recent. They formed below the sea 250 million years ago. Fossils of reptiles and insects that were alive millions of years before people existed have been found in these rocks.

The rocks halfway down the canyon are 400 million years old; some contain fish remains. Lower down, in rocks 500 million years old, there are only shellfish and worm fossils. Right at the bottom of the canyon, the rocks are 2 billion years old. Life may have existed on Earth then, but no traces of living things have been found.

*cliffs collapse as softer rocks are worn away*

*the Colorado River may be up to 30 million years old*

*muddy river carries soil and small pieces of rock (this shows it is eroding the surface of the land)*

# The middle river

As a river gets farther from its source, more tributaries join it. The amount of water and material in the river increases. The land slopes more gently and the river starts to cut sideways into the land, rather than downward. The riverbed is no longer littered with pebbles and boulders. Instead, the water carries sand, mud and small stones, and the bed becomes lined with a smooth layer of mud and silt.

##  Cutting a smooth course

At this stage, the river carries its load suspended in the water. It also begins to swing from side to side, cutting into some banks and drifting away from others. There are no obstacles such as rapids, so the river's course becomes smoother and more regular.

△ *This is the middle section of the Mekong River in Cambodia. The river carries a lot of mud and silt.*

▷ *This is a river in its middle course, flowing through tropical rain forest. The river winds its way across a flat valley floor and thick rain forest grows to the river's edge.*

## MAKE A FLOW METER

**You will need:** strip of wood, dowel, funnel, balsa wood, plasticine, tape, thumbtack, glue, drill, paints, protractor, craft knife (ask an adult for help)

**1** Cut a balsa wood semicircle and paint it. Using a protractor, mark every 10° on one half.

**2** Glue the semicircle, or dial, to your wood strip, about a third of the way down.

**3** Drill a small hole in the dowel, about a third of the way along. Paint this third—this is your needle.

**4** With the thumbtack, attach the needle to the wood strip, just below the dial. Make sure it can swing freely.

**5** Make a stopper in the end of the funnel with plasticine. Tape or glue the funnel to the unpainted end of the needle. Paint the rest of your flow meter.

**6** Place the meter upright in the middle of a shallow stream (the funnel should face upstream). The flow of the river will make the needle move across the dial. The farther the needle moves toward the horizontal, the faster the flow. Test the flow closer to the river bank. Is there a difference?

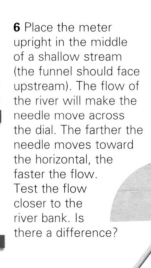

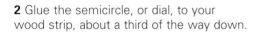

## 👫 Transport and trade

In many parts of the world, people rely on the middle river for food, transport and trade. In the rain forest, people also rely on the trees and vegetation that grow to the river's edge. Rain forests contain valuable trees such as teak, mahogany and rosewood. Sometimes, areas of the forest are cleared by cutting down the trees. Logs are floated downriver and loaded onto ships where the river meets the sea. Once the trees and vegetation are cleared away, the thin soil is easily washed away by heavy rain. Then the land cannot be used for growing crops or more trees.

## ⛰ Speed of flow

Along the middle river, the channel is deep and lined with smooth mud and silt. There is less friction between the river and the riverbed because there are no boulders or stones to slow down the flow of the river. The water flows fastest in the center of the river channel near the surface, where there is least friction.

*floodwaters leave mud and silt on the riverbank*

*village built on higher land near river*

*meandering river*

*river drops material on inside bend to make a beach*

*trees cut down for timber cause more soil to be washed into the river*

*sawmill pollutes the river*

# The middle river

 **The changing course**
The path of the middle river is always changing as it cuts sideways into the land and starts to deposit its load. Loops, called meanders, and **oxbow lakes** are typical features of this part of the river. During a storm, meanders stop river water flowing easily. This causes water to build up in places, and may lead to flooding.

 **How meanders form**
Rivers twist and turn naturally as they flow over the land creating meanders. These tend to form in places where there are wide, strong riverbanks. Large rivers, such as the Mississippi in the U.S., have meanders that are many miles across.

△ *This photograph shows an oxbow lake along the Manu River in the rain forest of Peru.*

cliff

bar

**1** As the river travels along more gently sloping land, it starts to curve across the valley floor. When rivers swing from side to side, they flow more slowly than when they flow in a straight line.

**2** Over time, the meander becomes bigger. As the river slowly cuts away the bank on the outside curve, it leaves the material it is carrying on the inside curve. These ridges of sand and gravel are called bars.

**3** A wide swing forms along the path of the river. Gradually, a cliff starts to form on the outside bend where the river has cut into the banks.

 **From meanders to oxbow lakes**
Oxbow lakes begin as meanders. As the river continues to wear away the bank on the outside bend of the meander, the river channel becomes more U-shaped. Eventually, the river cuts through the neck of the meander to make a new channel.

oxbow lake

**1** The river has formed a meander so wide that it is almost a circle. There is only a narrow strip of land separating the sections of the river channels.

**2** The river has cut through the "neck" of the meander and formed a new, straighter channel.

**3** As the river continues along its new path, it leaves behind a horseshoe-shaped lake called an oxbow lake. Over time, plants and vegetation will grow over this lake.

## ⛰ River terraces

When the surface of the land is pushed up by movements under the Earth, rivers cut down into the land. This also happens with a drop in the level of the lake or sea into which a river flows. A step-like strip is left behind on the sides of the valley, at a higher level than the new river channel. This is a river terrace. Terraces can also form if rainfall increases. The river becomes more powerful and cuts into the land.

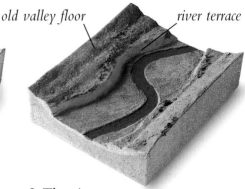

*old valley floor*     *river terrace*

**1** As the river meanders along the valley floor, the land may rise or the water level may drop. Then the river starts to cut down into the land.

**2** The river forms a new valley at a lower level. The old valley floor forms a river terrace on the valley sides. Over time, many terraces may form.

## THE GRADIENT TEST

**You will need** three bricks, small plastic window box, sheet of hardboard, jug, plasticine, plastic cup, water

**1** Arrange the bricks, hardboard and window box as shown above. Pour water down the steep slope and watch.

**Result:** over a steep gradient, you will see that water takes the most direct path to the window box (sea).

**2** Reduce the height of the bricks to make a shallow slope. Make a small hole near the bottom of the plastic cup and place it at the top of the board. Make a narrow channel with the plasticine and press it around the hole and onto the board. Pour the water into the cup and watch.

**Result:** over a shallow gradient, water begins to meander and travels more slowly on its journey to the sea.

# The middle river

## 👫 Living along the middle river

In **developed countries**, such as those of Europe or North America, the middle river is used in all sorts of ways. Towns and cities have grown up in places where it is easy to cross the river. A flat valley floor is ideal for building roads and railroads, while the river is an efficient way to carry people and goods from place to place.

## 🏔 Soil fertility

The success of farming along the middle river often depends on the soil. Some types of soil are more suitable for growing crops than others. To test soil, farmers find out its pH (potential hydrogen) value. This is measured on a scale from 0–14. Neutral is 7, anything less than 7 is acidic, and anything greater is alkaline. Some crops grow better in slightly acid soil, whereas others prefer more alkaline soil.

### TEST SOIL pH

    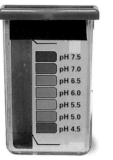 

**You will need** a pH testing kit from your local garden center, jug, glass, distilled water, pipette, soil

**1** Place some soil in a glass and add some distilled water. Stir and leave the mixture to settle.

**2** Take a sample from the glass with a pipette and add to your testing kit. Open the capsule that comes with the testing kit and add it to the water and soil mixture in the kit. Replace the lid on the testing kit and shake well for about a minute.

**3** Match the color of the mixture to the pH value on the kit.

**Result:** the redder the color, the more acid the soil; the blacker the color, the more alkaline the soil. Neutral is pH 7.0.

## 👫 Early settlements

Thousands of years ago, when people first lived in towns and cities, they chose sites near rivers for their settlements. They needed water for drinking, as well as for farming and transport. The first great civilizations all developed along rivers—the Nile in Egypt, the Huang He River in China, the Tigris-Euphrates in Iraq and the Indus in Pakistan. These river valleys all had something in common: a fertile **floodplain** with rich fields for farming and fresh water to supply a growing population.

## 👫 River transport

Until a hundred and fifty years ago, there were no railroads, and many roads were simply muddy tracks. The safest way to transport heavy goods was by barge and boat along rivers. In many parts of the world today, rivers are still important highways for moving goods. To keep river channels deep enough for large boats to use, dredgers clear away the silt and mud.

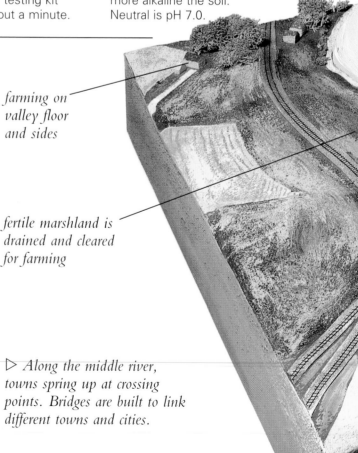

*farming on valley floor and sides*

*fertile marshland is drained and cleared for farming*

▷ *Along the middle river, towns spring up at crossing points. Bridges are built to link different towns and cities.*

△ *The town of Cochem grew at a bridging point along the middle course of the Moselle River in Germany.*

## 🏔 The middle river valley

The model below shows some of the features you might see on rivers such as the Rhine or the Danube in Europe, or the St Lawrence in Canada. The river winds its way across a flat valley floor, dropping some of its load to form bars on the inside curves of meanders. Dams and lakes farther upstream control the flow of the river. The river and its valley are vital for settlements, farming and transport.

*river has worn away most of the valley sides to make a flat valley bottom*

*river is used to transport raw materials and goods to and from factories*

*river is used for sailing, fishing and water-skiing*

*cities, factories and power stations may pollute the water in the river*

# The human water cycle

We need fresh drinking water in order to survive, but we also need water for washing, cooking and heating. Most of our fresh water comes from rivers and reservoirs. In many countries, water is cleaned before and after it is used to remove dirt and germs. As there is only a certain amount of fresh water on Earth, we need to keep our rivers clean if we are to continue taking water from them.

## Taking water from rivers

The cycle begins when we take water from rivers. Sticks, leaves and any large objects are cleared from the water before it is pumped to a reservoir. From the reservoir, the water passes to a treatment plant. It settles in tanks lined with sand and gravel, which trap the dirt. A chemical called chlorine is added to kill the germs, making the water clean and safe to drink. Finally, the water is either stored or pumped directly to homes and factories along pipes under the roads.

## Cleanup operation

Once it has been used, dirty water goes into huge underground pipes called sewers that carry the water to the sewage treatment plant. The water is cleaned by a kind of **bacteria** that eat the germs and dirt, leaving only gases and water behind. At this stage the water is clean enough to be pumped back into the river. Every glass of water we drink has been used hundreds of times before as part of the endless human water cycle.

▽ *This model shows the "human water cycle": how we take water from the river, clean it, use it, and then clean it again before returning it to the river.*

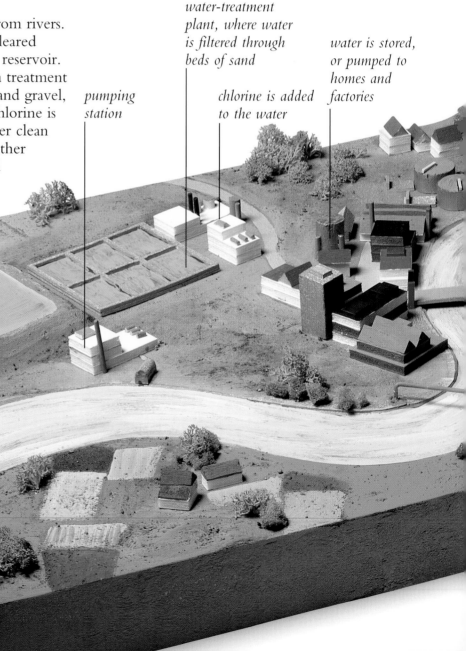

water-treatment plant, where water is filtered through beds of sand

water is stored, or pumped to homes and factories

pumping station

chlorine is added to the water

storage reservoir

**WATER FILTER TEST**

**You will need** plastic bottle, scissors, sphagnum (garden) moss, sand, gravel, soil, leaves, jug, water, glass, bradawl

**1** Cut the bottom off the bottle. Carefully make a small hole in the bottle top with a bradawl, then replace the bottle top.

**2** Pour some sand into the bottle. Then add some moss. Build up three layers of moss and sand. Finally, add a layer of gravel.

**3** Mix some sand, gravel, soil, leaves and water separately in the jug.

**4** Balance the bottle on top of the glass and pour in the water mixture.

**Result:** the sand and moss will trap most of the debris. The water in the glass should be almost clear, perhaps with some sand particles remaining.

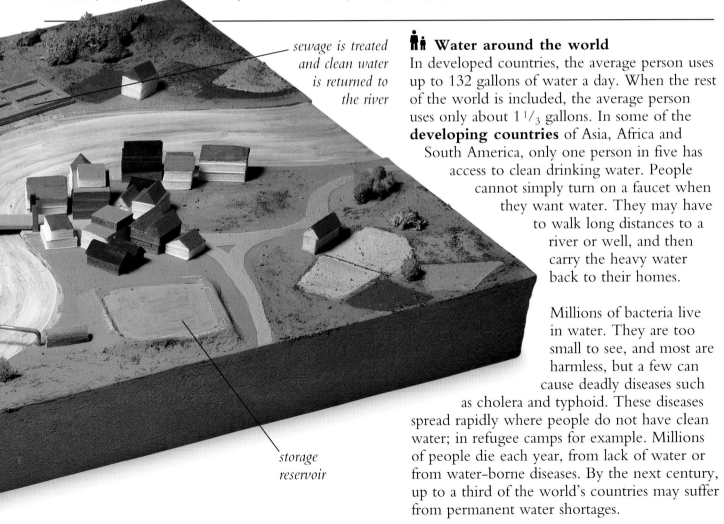

*sewage is treated and clean water is returned to the river*

*storage reservoir*

**Water around the world**

In developed countries, the average person uses up to 132 gallons of water a day. When the rest of the world is included, the average person uses only about 1 1/3 gallons. In some of the **developing countries** of Asia, Africa and South America, only one person in five has access to clean drinking water. People cannot simply turn on a faucet when they want water. They may have to walk long distances to a river or well, and then carry the heavy water back to their homes.

Millions of bacteria live in water. They are too small to see, and most are harmless, but a few can cause deadly diseases such as cholera and typhoid. These diseases spread rapidly where people do not have clean water; in refugee camps for example. Millions of people die each year, from lack of water or from water-borne diseases. By the next century, up to a third of the world's countries may suffer from permanent water shortages.

37

# Farming on the lower river

Near the end of its journey, a river flows across an almost flat plain toward its mouth. This is part of the lower river. Here, the river is wide and no longer cuts down into the land. It still wears away its banks though, and makes a wide, flat valley floor called a floodplain. At this stage, the river deposits fine mud on the riverbed and riverbanks. When the river floods, the mud spreads all over the floodplain.

## 🏔 The fertile floodplain

After heavy rain, or when snow melts in the mountains, more water suddenly pours into the river. All this extra water in the lower river can cause the river to burst its banks and overflow onto the floodplain. When this happens, the water spreads out in a thin sheet over the valley floor.

As the river starts to slow down, it drops the heaviest part of its load (coarse sand) first. This builds up on the riverbanks to form broad walls called levees. Finer sediment, such as mud, is washed out onto the flat valley floor. After many floods, layers of this sediment, called **alluvium**, build up into fertile land that is good for farming.

## FLOOD A RIVER VALLEY

△ *Lower river meandering across a wide, flat floodplain.*

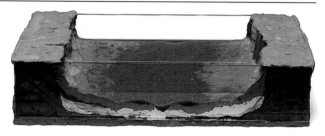

△ *As the river floods, fertile mud spreads over the valley.*

**You will need** baseboard, tape, two sheets of Plexiglass or glass, four bricks, sand, jug, water, blue food coloring, colored plasticine: brown for bedrock, white for river channel, green for vegetation, yellow for sand

**1** Position the bricks on either side of the baseboard. Cover them with layers of plasticine to make a steep-sided valley as shown above.

**2** Carve out a meandering river channel and line it with white plasticine. Add yellow plasticine (for sand deposits) on the inner bends of the river.

**3** Make your river valley watertight by pressing the sheets of Plexiglass or glass into the plasticine at each end. Fix with tape if necessary. Next, fill a jug with water and add a little blue food coloring.

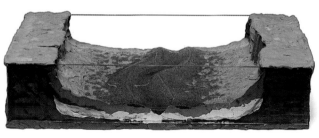

△ *Raised banks, or levees, form on both sides of the river where sand and gravel have been deposited.*

**4** Mix some sand with the water. Pour the mixture slowly into the course of the river, as shown at left. The river will begin to rise over its banks and flood the surrounding land.

**5** Carefully remove one of the Plexiglass sheets and allow the water to drain away. The sand in the water (representing alluvium) should be spread thinly all over the floodplain.

**6** Replace the Plexiglass sheet. Pour some more water into the river channel. This time, the water should flow between the newly formed banks, or levees.

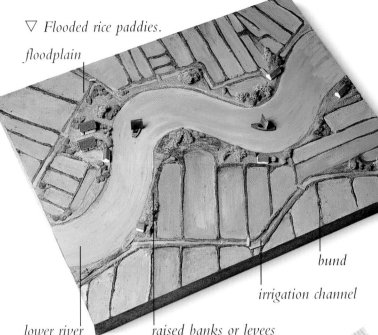

▽ *Flooded rice paddies.*

*floodplain*

*bund*

*irrigation channel*

*lower river*     *raised banks or levees*

### 🌸 A watering machine

A shadoof is a simple device used in many places to lift water from rivers to fields at a higher level. It is a long lever with a bucket on one end and a weight on the other. The farmer dips the bucket into the river, swings it around and empties the water onto the field.

### 👫 Rice farming in China

China has only 7 per cent of the world's farmland, yet it tries to grow enough to feed its huge population which is 20 per cent of the world's total. Rice is the staple food and it is grown near rivers as it needs plenty of water.

River water is fed to the rice fields, or paddies, via a series of irrigation channels. Little walls of stone or soil, called bunds, hold in the water, and small sluice gates control the flow to the fields. As the rice grows, the water level is checked and topped up if necessary. In China, land is never wasted. Flooded paddy fields are sometimes used for fish farming, and crops of sugar cane and mulberries are grown on banks between the fields.

### 👫 Danger—flooding!

Many people live on river valley floors despite the risk of flood, either because the land is so fertile or because they have nowhere else to live. In Bangladesh, most of the land is floodplain. Each year many people lose their lives and their homes in floods there.

## MAKE A SHADOOF

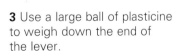

*funnel*

**5** Fill the funnel with water. Now swing your shadoof around and pull out the stop to release the water.

**You will need** strip of wood 23 in. long, piece of wood 7 x 4 in., 8 in. length of $\frac{1}{3}$ in. dowel, funnel, plasticine, string, 1 in. length of $\frac{1}{8}$ in. dowel, hand drill

**1** Drill a $\frac{1}{3}$ in. hole in the center of the wooden board, and a $\frac{1}{8}$ in. hole through one end of the $\frac{1}{3}$ in. dowel. Drill two $\frac{1}{8}$ in. holes in the long wooden strip (lever) as shown above.

**2** Push the long dowel into the baseboard and secure with plasticine (it should still be able to turn freely). Pass the small dowel (pivot) through the hole in the large dowel and through the hole in the lever as shown at right.

**3** Use a large ball of plasticine to weigh down the end of the lever.

**4** Make two small holes in the funnel as above. Thread string through the holes and tie as shown. Thread the loose end of string through the hole in the lever and tie around the pivot. Make a stop in the funnel with plasticine.

*lever*

*pivot*

*weight*

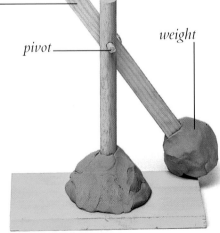

# River deltas

Most rivers end their journey when they flow into the sea or a lake. The river slows down and deposits the sediment it is carrying. Heavy grains of sand and gravel drop to the bottom. Lighter particles of fine silt and clay are carried farther out to sea, or into the lake. Gradually, the sediment spreads out to form a new piece of land with gently sloping sides. This is called a delta. This word comes from the Greek letter △ (delta), after the shape of the Nile Delta in Egypt.

## 👫 Farming and settlement

Deltas build up from layers of mineral-rich sediments. For centuries, people have farmed the flat land of deltas. Important cities are often built on or near deltas, such as Shanghai on the Yangtze Delta, Alexandria on the Nile Delta, and New Orleans on the Mississippi Delta. As deltas grow, cities may end up farther away from the sea.

## 🏔 Estuaries

Sometimes the sea level rises and floods the mouth of a river. Seawater drowns the river valley, creating a long funnel shape in from the coast, called an **estuary**. Estuaries are not filled in with sediment like deltas, but they do have lots of rich mud that contains food for wildlife.

▷ *When the river reaches the delta, it splits into branching channels called* **distributaries***. They carry water over the surface of the delta.*

*farms on the edge of a fertile river delta*

*water spills over the distributaries, dropping sediment that forms levees*

*surface of the delta gradually builds up as more sediment is deposited*

*sediment deposited under the sea beyond the edge of the delta*

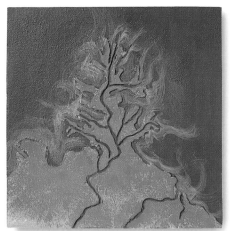
*bird's-foot delta*

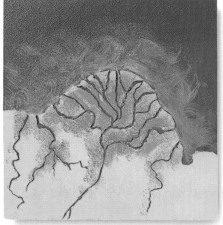
*arcuate delta*

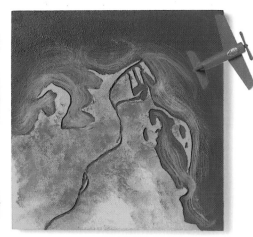
*cuspate delta*

## 🏔 Shapes of deltas

The shape of a delta depends on how much water and sediment is carried by the river, and how fast the water is flowing. It also depends on the speed and strength of the sea's waves, currents and tides.

When a lot of sediment is carried out into calm seawater, a bird's-foot delta forms. The distributaries carry long "toes" of sediment out into the sea. The Mississippi Delta is shaped like this.

An arcuate delta is shaped like a triangle. It forms when a river meets the sea in a place where the waves, currents and tides are not strong. The deltas of the Nile, Indus and Rhône are shaped like this.

When a river drops sediment onto a straight shoreline with strong waves, a cuspate delta is formed. Waves force the sediment to spread outward in both directions from the river's mouth, making a pointed tooth shape, with curved sides.

## DELTA EXPERIMENT

**You will need** large plastic garden tray, bricks, shingle (small stones), sand, water, blue food coloring, jug, two white wooden boards as shown below

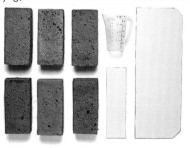

**1** Arrange the bricks in the tray as shown at right (they represent the land). Pour the shingle between the bricks. Place the narrower strip of wood on top of the shingle, between the bricks, to form a ramp.

**2** Use the larger piece of wood as a seabed. Place some shingle at the base of the ramp, between the bricks (neck of land), to make a shingle beach.

**3** Half-fill the tray with water (to represent the sea). Mix some sand in a jug with colored water and pour into the back of the tray to create a river.

◁ *The sand deposits have formed a triangular, or arcuate, delta.*

**Result:** as the sediment (sand) flows down the river channel, the delta should grow and spread into a fan shape.

# Flood control

Floods occur when the water in a river suddenly rises and the banks cannot contain it. In large floods, the river may be ten times deeper and carry a hundred times more water than usual. Floods can be caused by natural events, such as high tides, heavy rainstorms or melting snow. They can also be caused by cutting down trees that soak up rainfall, or by draining marshy land into a river.

△ *The Thames Barrier has 10 movable steel gates that can be raised to make a 59 foot-high wall.*

## Preventing damage

Natural floods are impossible to stop, but it is possible to reduce the damage they cause to people and property. Building walls or levees along rivers and coasts is one solution. Others include dredging the river to make it wider and deeper, and building reservoirs to hold extra water.

## The Thames Barrier

Mechanical barriers can prevent floodwaters from damaging towns and cities. London, England, is in danger of being flooded when there is a high tide or a storm. This is because the sea level is rising and the land is slowly sinking. Movable barriers can be raised to stop the river water flowing upstream.

## BUILD A THAMES BARRIER

### You will need
shingle (small stones), plasticine, glass or Plexiglass tank, 8 in. length of dowel, two gutter stops, 13 in. length of rain gutter, hand drill, wood (pine): base: 8 x 3 in., two uprights: 6 x 2 in., paints

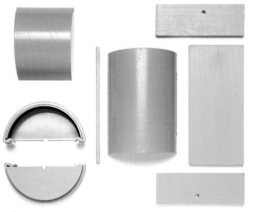

### Note:
measurements of barrier will vary depending on the size of your tank.

**1** Drill two 1/5 in. holes in the uprights, as shown. For the support, glue the upright pieces to the wooden base, as shown at right. Paint the support.

**2** Cut a 7 in. length of rain gutter. Make a notch in each of the gutter stops as shown above. Attach the gutter stops to the ends of the rain gutter to make your barrier.

**3** Slide the barrier and the dowel into the drilled holes in the gutter stops and uprights. Next, cut a 6 1/5 in. section of gutter. Slide it underneath the barrier as shown at right.

**4** Make a watertight seal with plasticine between the second piece of rain gutter and the base. Place the barrier and a bed of shingle in the tank. Make another seal between the support and the tank (as shown opposite). Slip the barrier into the upright position.

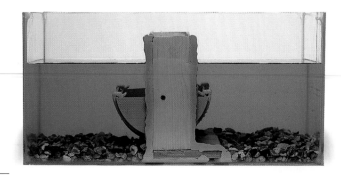

**5** Pour a little water into the left side (to represent the river flowing downstream). Fill the right side of the tank with water (incoming tide). The barrier stops the tide running upstream and flooding the river. Now lower the barrier so that it lies flat (as shown below). When the level of the river is the same on both sides, ships can pass.

## 👫 Holding back the Mississippi

Severe flooding often occurs along the Mississippi River in the U.S. To help control the flooding, 3,600 miles of levees have been built from soil, rock and sand. The soil is usually taken from "borrow pits" around the river. The large pits later fill in with water and become human-made lakes.

In Bangladesh and other developing countries where floods claim many lives each year, there is not much money available for flood control. Levees are often built from whatever materials people can find—soil, wood, old tires and corrugated iron.

## 🏔 Flood-control problems

Building levees can cause problems. If a river does not flood, then fertile sediment is no longer spread over the plain, so the land is not as good for farming. Also, sections of rivers with levees hold more water. This sometimes leads to water being forced into unprotected sections downstream.

*sandbags for
extra protection*

*borrow pit*

*raised
levee*

*tree and plant
roots soak up water
and help to bind the soil*

△ *Levees built on the banks of the
Mississippi River.*

▽ *The raised barrier holds back the incoming tide.*

# Managing rivers

Rivers and the land beside them are used for farming, industry, energy, transport, water supply and recreation. They are also a home for wildlife. Sometimes people upset the balance of rivers by taking too much water from them, by polluting the water and by overfishing. People also try to control floods by changing the river's course. Often, rivers flow through several countries and people do not always agree on the best way of handling the river's resources.

△ *Keeping rivers clean and free from pollution makes them safe for spawning salmon and other wildlife.*

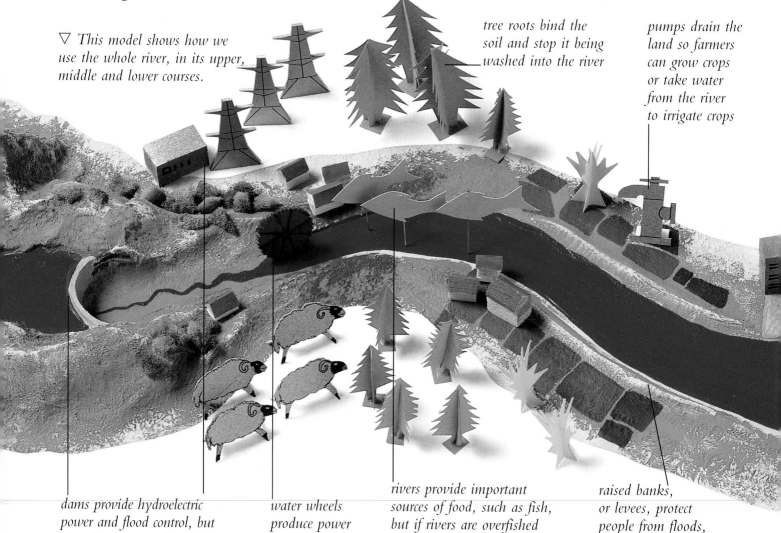

▽ *This model shows how we use the whole river, in its upper, middle and lower courses.*

*tree roots bind the soil and stop it being washed into the river*

*pumps drain the land so farmers can grow crops or take water from the river to irrigate crops*

*dams provide hydroelectric power and flood control, but alter the amount of water and sediment in the river*

*water wheels produce power from flowing water*

*rivers provide important sources of food, such as fish, but if rivers are overfished and the water is polluted, the supply will dwindle*

*raised banks, or levees, protect people from floods, but force more water downstream*

## 👫 People and pollution

Every day, we take about four-fifths of the world's freshwater that is stored in rivers and in rocks underground. As the world's population grows, water shortages may be more of a problem than food shortages in the next century.

Making sure that people have clean water to drink is another problem. In developing countries, pollution control is very expensive and the river water may be dirty and dangerous to people's health. People may not be able to afford to clean river water before and after they use it. Developed countries also face the problems of pollution—especially if industries are allowed to dump waste into the river.

## 🏔 👫 Managing the river

People throughout the world depend on rivers, but managing them can cause problems. In order to avoid flooding disasters in the future, it is important to understand why rivers flow the way they do, and what happens when we alter them.

Sometimes, rivers and the sediment they carry are too heavily managed. Dams, barriers and banks control the river in a very unnatural way. They may give protection from floods and other disasters for a while, but over time rivers always fight back, trying to take the easiest path across land. If we are to make the best possible use of rivers, we need to look at the river as a whole, and not just a section at a time.

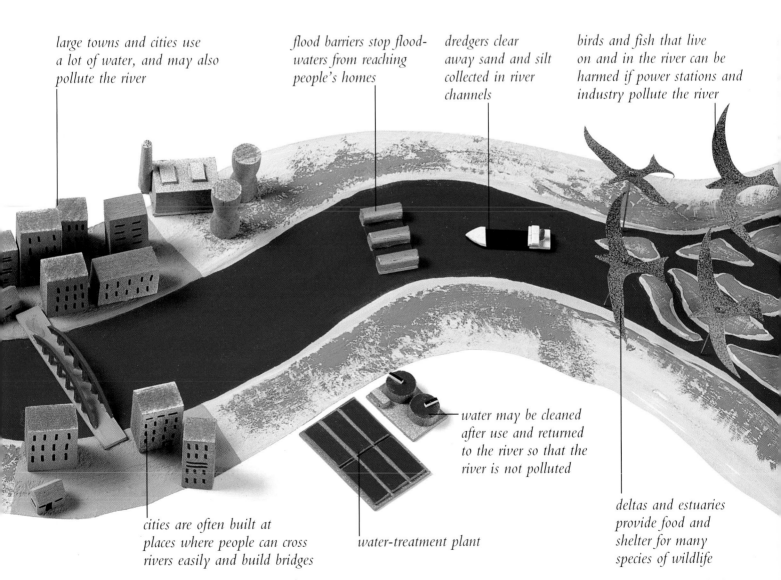

*large towns and cities use a lot of water, and may also pollute the river*

*flood barriers stop flood-waters from reaching people's homes*

*dredgers clear away sand and silt collected in river channels*

*birds and fish that live on and in the river can be harmed if power stations and industry pollute the river*

*water may be cleaned after use and returned to the river so that the river is not polluted*

*cities are often built at places where people can cross rivers easily and build bridges*

*water-treatment plant*

*deltas and estuaries provide food and shelter for many species of wildlife*

# Glossary

**alluvium** Material such as fine sand, silt and clay that is deposited by the river over the land, especially in the lower river and on the delta.

**aquifer** An area of underground permeable rock that absorbs and stores water.

**atmosphere** The air surrounding the Earth. It is made up of a mixture of gases.

**bacteria** Tiny organisms that can be seen only under a microscope. They are used to break down soil and sewage, but they also cause serious diseases in people, animals and plants.

**canyon** A large, deep river valley with steep sides.

**contour line** A line on a map joining a series of points that are the same height above sea level.

**dam** A large wall or bank built across a river to hold back water. A dam can be used to control the water flowing in a river and prevent flooding. It can also be used to direct the water towards water wheels or turbines to generate power.

**delta** An area of flat land near the sea or a lake that is made up of sediment deposited by the river.

**developed countries** Wealthy countries, such as those in North America or parts of Europe or Australasia, which have developed a strong industrial base and a high standard of living for most of the people there.

**developing countries** Poor countries in parts of Africa, Asia and South America which are trying to create an industrial base and improve the economic and social conditions for their people.

**distributaries** Small, shifting river channels on a river delta that carry water and sediment away from the main river and spread it over the delta.

**drainage basin** The total area of land that is drained by a river and its tributaries.

**drainage pattern** The way a river and its tributaries are arranged on land, seen from a bird's-eye viewpoint.

**erosion** Wearing away of the land by water, wind and ice.

**estuary** The wide mouth of a river where fresh water meets the sea.

**floodplain** A broad, flat area of land on either side of the lower river. It is covered with sand, silt and clay deposited by the river when it floods.

**fossil** The remains of a prehistoric plant or animal which have undergone a chemical change and been preserved in rock.

**geology** Studying the Earth's history by looking at the rocks that make up the Earth's crust.

**glacier** A large mass of ice that forms when snow is packed down hard in a hollow on a mountainside.

**groundwater** All the water underneath the ground that fills cracks, crevices and pores in rocks and soil.

**hydroelectric power** Electricity that is generated by turbines driven by water falling down from a height.

**interlocking spurs** Tongues of land on the sides of a river valley around which the river winds. When the points of the spurs are eroded by the river, they become truncated.

**irrigate** To carry water to crops and pastures by artificial means. Almost 20 per cent of the world's cropland is now irrigated.

**load** The sediment carried by a river. There are three types of load—solute load (material that is dissolved in the water), suspended load (fine particles floating in the water), and bedload (large, heavy particles that move along the river bed).

**lower river** The last section of a river's course where it flows across an almost level plain to its mouth. The river deposits material rather than eroding the land.

**meander** A natural curve or bend in a river, often occurring in the middle course.

**middle river** The central section of a river's course linking the upper and lower river. The river cuts sideways into the land, carries finer sediments and also deposits some material.

**oxbow lake** A meander that has been cut off from the river to form a horseshoe-shaped lake.

**permeable** A rock that allows water to pass through it is called permeable. Some rocks, such as limestone, let water pass through them easily. Impermeable rocks like slate, do not.

**porous** A rock or soil that can hold water is known as porous. This depends on the number of pores in the rock or soil. Chalk is a porous rock.

**rapids** A stretch of rough and fast-flowing water in the upper river. A series of rapids are called cataracts.

**reservoir** An artificial lake storing water for drinking, electricity or irrigation.

**river valley** A long, narrow hollow in the Earth's surface in which a river flows. In the upper river, valleys are narrow and steep-sided. Lower down the river's course, valleys are wider, with gently sloping sides.

**sediment** Loose, solid particles of rocks or living things that are carried along and deposited by the river.

**sedimentary rock** A type of rock, such as chalk or sandstone. It is formed from loose sediments, vegetation or fossils that have been deposited in layers over millions of years.

**silt** Very fine grains of sediment that are carried and deposited by a river.

**stalactite** An icicle-shaped deposit of minerals that hangs down from the ceiling of a cave.

**stalagmite** A cone-shaped mass of minerals deposited on cave floors, often directly below a stalactite.

**statistics** Facts given in the form of figures.

**tributary** A stream or small river flowing into a larger river or stream.

**upper river** The first part of a river's course, starting at the source of the river. The river cuts down deeply into the land and may form gorges.

**water table** The level to which the ground is full, or saturated with water. The water table rises after rainfall and falls during dry weather.

**water vapor** Water that is held in the Earth's atmosphere in the form of a gas.

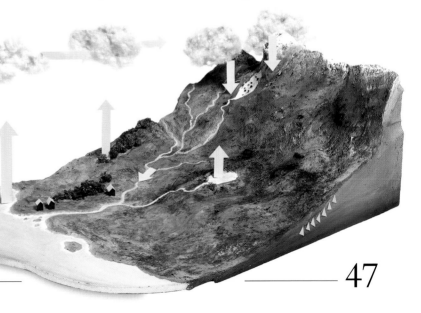